The JOURNEY of YORK

The Unsung Hero of the Lewis and Clark Expedition

by Hasan Davis   illustrated by Alleanna Harris

content consulting by
James J. Holmberg
Curator of Collections
The Filson Historical Society
Louisville, Kentucky

CAPSTONE EDITIONS
a capstone imprint

Long before Thomas Jefferson became America's third president, he dreamed of western exploration. Once elected, he made it one of his priorities. In January 1803 he sent a secret message to Congress requesting funding for a modest expedition to explore the western continent from the frontier to the Pacific Ocean. The purpose of this journey was to establish new trade routes; document the flora, fauna, and landscape; and inform the western tribes of American Indians that they were now a part of the United States.

President Jefferson called the exploring team his "Corps of Discovery." It was Jefferson's hope that they would find a water route to the Pacific. Expecting it to be a perilous journey, Jefferson picked Meriwether Lewis to lead the expedition. Lewis was Jefferson's private secretary, an officer in the military, and a frontiersman. The president had complete faith in Lewis's ability to lead such an important mission.

After accepting the assignment, Captain Lewis contacted his old army commander, Captain William Clark, and enlisted him as co-commander of the expedition. Clark was an experienced soldier and frontiersman as well, with a reputation for being a leader other men would follow.

Captain Lewis wanted "some good hunters, stout, healthy, unmarried men, accustomed to the woods, and capable of bearing bodily fatigue in a pretty considerable degree." The captains recruited twenty-seven volunteers for the mission.

When Captain Clark accepted co-command of the expedition, he ordered York, his slave, to prepare for the trip. York was born into slavery in the early 1770s, a time in America when it was legal for one person to own another. He was the property of John Clark, William Clark's father. From an early age, York spent his time with William and was ordered to serve and protect him with his own life. When John Clark died, he left York and several other slaves to William. As property, York did not have a choice in whether he would volunteer for Jefferson's dangerous mission. Slaves did not have choices.

In May 1804 Captain Lewis, Captain Clark, and twenty-eight men set out from St. Louis, Missouri, in three boats with the goal of reaching the Pacific Ocean.

All but one of those men were volunteers.

Printed in the United States   6007

This is his story.

Fort Clatsop,
Oregon

Great Falls,
Montana

Fort Mandan,
North Dakota

ROCKY MOUNTAINS

MISSOURI RIVER

Council on the Bluffs,
Nebraska

St. Louis,
Missouri

October 1803, Louisville, Kentucky

"York!" Master Clark called. I walked over to where he was packing his journals. "Run to the dock and remind those soldiers to pack the keelboat just as Captain Lewis has ordered."

My hesitation was obvious, but I ran to deliver the message.

"Why does Clark keep sending his boy to tell us what to do?" muttered one soldier.

"When did it become acceptable for a slave to order a white man around?" another barked.

"York," a third man interrupted. It was Charles Floyd. "Thank you for the message. You can assure the captain that we will take care of everything according to specifications."

We left Louisville and headed for St. Louis, Missouri. The hardest part was not knowing if I would ever make it home to my family. I didn't volunteer to be one of the president's "men of discovery." It wasn't my decision to leave my wife and loved ones. I am a slave, and slaves don't get to decide.

The captains said that we would spend the winter in St. Louis, recruiting our last members and preparing for the journey. We would be rowing, poling, and pulling upstream against the current of the Missouri River. We would be seeking safe passage from Indian nations. We would be climbing the highest mountains. It would not be easy.

July 4, 1804, (present) Atchison, Kansas

After pushing up the Missouri River for many months, we prepared for Independence Day. The whole camp was full of energy. We would be the first Americans west of the Mississippi River to celebrate this important day.

"I believe this is what we fought for, York," Sergeant Floyd said to me. "All Americans working side by side to build a great nation. I was raised believing that this is what American independence should look like."

Floyd was different from most of the other soldiers. He grew up in Kentucky, a slave state, but his family did not believe that God intended one man to own another. They had moved across the Ohio River to Indiana, a free territory.

Today was the nation's twenty-eighth Independence Day. I had been alive for all of them. But I did not have independence. If there were more men like Charles Floyd in the world, I could hope that one day that sweet bell of liberty would ring for me.

August 1804, (present) Omaha, Nebraska

George Drouillard, the son of a French man and a Shawnee woman, was our best interpreter. He could speak English and French, and he knew how to communicate with most Indians we met, either with words or by using his hands. We called it "sign talking."

When we encountered our first nation, a small gathering of Otoe-Missouria Indians, the leader we met started talking right to me. Captain Lewis stepped in and asked Drouillard to explain to the Indian that I was not the leader of our group.

Later, at the council on the bluffs, the captains met with leaders from the Otoe-Missouria to present gifts and declare America's claim on their land. I asked Drouillard to explain what had happened earlier, when the Indian leader tried to speak with me. He explained that the man, Chief of the Bear Clan, had thought I was his spirit brother. He didn't know why I failed to recognize him.

It was then that I realized that though these Indians had met white men before, they had likely never seen a black man like me.

August 20, 1804, (present) Sioux City, Iowa

A good man died today. My friend, Sergeant Charles Floyd, has been sickly for more than a week. Though yesterday he seemed much improved, today he is gone. There was nothing we could do. Captain Lewis used every bit of his skill but could not save him.

I sat with my friend as he died, and I cried.

Captain Lewis performed a beautiful service with all the honors of war. He named a river and the small bluff where we buried him after Sergeant Floyd.

October 1804, Fort Mandan, (present) North Dakota

Each time we met a new Indian nation, the captains would explain to them that they were now part of a new tribe called the United States, and that they had a new, great chief called the president. They also had a duty now to protect the president's "warriors" . . . or suffer for it. Then, in case there was any misunderstanding, one of our Corps would demonstrate for the Indians the power of our new rifle.

Our experience with the Sioux nations during the previous month did not go as well as the captains had hoped. The powerful Sioux were unimpressed by the captains' speeches, gifts, and displays of military might.

We hoped things would go better with the Mandan and Hidatsa people and arrived in their villages with plans to build a winter camp. Our interpreters' skills had gotten us this far, but we would need someone familiar with the Indians of the far western nations to complete the journey. The captains met Toussaint Charbonneau, a French man who said he knew the ways and the languages of the western tribes. He also had a Shoshone wife named Sacagawea who could help. He said that, for a price, he could lead us to the ocean.

That bitterly cold winter we also met One-Eye, chief of the Hidatsa Indians. Chief One-Eye had earlier refused to honor us with a visit. The Hidatsa had supported the British during the Revolution, and after that loss, Chief One-Eye had little trust left for white men.

But he heard intriguing tales of a black man, and curiosity finally drove him to visit our encampment, demanding to see me.

I stood in front of him as he licked his fingers and touched my skin. He said he thought it was another trick by the white men. When my color didn't come off, when he saw that I was black the way God intended, he proclaimed that I must be an important man. He treated me with respect and called me "Big Medicine." After his visit, our relations with Chief One-Eye and the Hidatsa people improved.

From then on, whenever we encountered a new nation, Captain Clark would call me forward and display me to his advantage. I would strip my shirt and perform great feats of strength or dance on my hands. My strength and the color of my skin—my "big medicine"—were used by Captain Clark to persuade the Indians of America's might.

November 1804, Fort Mandan

Charbonneau and Sacagawea joined us within Fort Mandan. Everyone called her his wife, but I heard how this teenage girl had been stolen from her family. Charbonneau bought Sacagawea in trade and made her his wife. I think that is why she and I became so close. She was the only other one out there who knew like I knew what it meant to be called the property of another.

Sacagawea gave birth to baby Jean Baptiste Charbonneau over the winter. Captain Clark gave him the nickname Pomp. Seeing this mother and child was a beautiful but painful reminder of the family I was forced to leave behind. I took it upon myself to protect Sacagawea and Pomp. I would keep them alive at any cost.

April 1805, Fort Mandan, and June–July 1805, (present) Great Falls, Montana

When the ice began to break along the river and the geese had been flying north for about three weeks, we left our winter camp at Fort Mandan. It was time to find a way to—and then through—the Rocky Mountains.

A few weeks in and still we had not reached the mountains. Captain Lewis scouted ahead. He returned with important news: "I have beheld the greatest site a man could ever see in the great falls ahead. What I thought would be an easy portage of perhaps one day will be much more difficult."

Captain Clark replied, "It is too late to turn back now. We either succeed or we perish in the attempt. We will face it like we have all the other obstacles. Together."

It took almost a month. We made wheels and axles to roll the canoes across eighteen miles. We had to find ways to lighten our load. We dug a hole to store supplies that we could not transport. They would be retrieved on the return journey. Together we worked ourselves to exhaustion and accomplished this task.

July 1805, Rocky Mountains

The Mandan had said that to cross the mountains we must have good horses, good supplies, and a man who knew the way through. They told us that the Shoshone Indians could provide all three. The Shoshone lived beyond the waterfalls. We spent the next few weeks that summer searching for them.

While we were searching, Captain Clark bestowed an honor on me. Throughout our journey, the captains made it a point to name the natural wonders we encountered. Some they named after our Corps members, as with the Floyd River. This day they named a group of islands after me—York's Eight Islands. That name meant a great deal to me and made me believe that the captains valued my efforts. It let me dare hope that my future might be different.

September 1805, Bitterroot Mountains, (present) Idaho

We found the Shoshone, and, as the Mandan had said, they provided us
with horses, supplies, and a guide to lead us. We set out. But even with
the guide and supplies, we were not prepared for the snowstorm that
struck once we began to cross the mountains. We lost our path. The
conditions got so bad, and we became so hungry, that we were forced
to kill and eat our horses. Everyone believed we were dying.

Captain Clark decided that smaller groups of us might be able to make
our way through the mountains and reach the other side. There was no
doubt that I would be beside him on this important mission, and with
Sacagawea and Pomp counting on us, I was determined not to fail. Our
party pushed hard through the mountains until we reached the territory
of the Nez Perce Indians.

October 1805, (present) Orofino, Idaho

We traded with the Nez Perce for roots, berries, and salmon. Then we made our way back to see how the others had fared. We were grateful to find that they had also survived the great mountain.

Once we were all safely out of the mountains, we stayed with the Nez Perce for several weeks to heal up and to build canoes for the last leg of our journey. Having little luck with our axes, the Nez Perce taught us how to use fire to hollow out tree trunks to build canoes. When all had recovered their strength, the captains said it was time to make for the ocean.

November 1805, (present) Washington State

On a cold, wet day in November, Captain Lewis stood at the bow, surveying the horizon. "Mount Hood!" he called out. It was the mountain British sailors had recorded in the 1790s when they visited the Pacific coast. Seeing it told us that we were indeed on the Columbia River and nearing the ocean.

As I strained my eyes, I was sure I saw the blue of the ocean in the distance too. After two hard years of wondering if I would ever see the ocean, there was our landmark, Mount Hood. Soon there were other signs. Gulls flew in the sky. The smell of salt water was in the air. When the captains were sure they had their first look at the ocean, they began shouting, "Ocean in view, ocean in view!"

We had finally made it to the Pacific. We had accomplished the mission given to us by President Jefferson. Today there was reason to celebrate.

November 1805, (present) Long Beach, Washington

The weather was rough and wet as we gathered on the north side of the river. The captains were discussing the best location to build our winter camp. One side was better for hunting, the other better for building and supplies. They decided to put to a vote which side of the Columbia River we would winter on. This surprised us all. Up until this point, the captains had made the decisions.

They went around and each person gave his vote. When they got to me, everyone stared as if expecting me to speak. I knew that in these United States we lived in, a slave had no right to vote. A black man never had the right to put his word up beside a white man's. I froze.

Captain Clark spoke. "It took every one of us to get this far. It took our blood, our sweat, and our whole heart to get us this far. . . . The way I see it, every man has earned the right to say where we go from here.

"York," he said, "it is time for you to vote."

So I voted, right there beside all those white men. I put my word up, and it counted for something.

November 1805, Fort Clatsop, (present) Astoria, Oregon

We decided to winter on the south side of the river, which had good elk
for hunting, and we started building our fort. We called it Fort Clatsop.
Captain Lewis named it to honor our new neighbors, the Clatsop Indians.

After that vote, even the dreary weather and cloudy days couldn't get me
down. In the next few weeks of building Fort Clatsop, I worked as hard as
any three men. Captain Clark said that I "pushed my body to exhaustion."
I just wanted to show the others how much I deserved that vote. In the
end, I think I proved my point.

December 25, 1805, Fort Clatsop

Captain Lewis called us to the campfire. "Our mission for the president is complete, a success," he said. "We will be going home soon and I will be making my report and introductions of the president's fine men of discovery, the men who sacrificed more than any patriot ought to volunteer for his nation. You are heroes. You made the president's dream come alive."

The fiddler started playing and Captain Lewis started calling the names like he was presenting us to President Jefferson. After each name there was a hoot and a holler. The fiddler played and we danced. We were having such a good time that no one even noticed—no one besides me—that when Captain Lewis called out the names of those brave heroes, my name was not included. That's when it first became clear that my return home would not be as celebrated as everyone else's.

March 23, 1806, Fort Clatsop

Spring has come and we will leave Fort Clatsop soon. Captain Clark is excited to return to what he calls "civilized" life: a life where he is my master and I his obedient slave.

I must return to such a life, for that is where my family is. I will tell them all that I have done. I worked hard every day and proved my right to cast a vote among other men. I have seen a world that few white men will ever dream of. I've climbed to the top of snow-capped mountains and swum rivers so swift that buffalo lost their footing. There are islands that bear my name. And I have walked among the first Americans, who welcomed me into their homes like a long-lost brother.

They called me Big Medicine, Gift from God, and Black Indian. And yet, I am still York. Just York. I ask you to remember the things I have done, so that when I am gone, my name, my voice, my story, do not die with me. These words are the only gift I have to give.

AUTHOR'S NOTE

They had been away from the eyes of the whole world almost three years—thousands of miles from civilization and lifetimes away from the inhumane system called "slavery." They returned to St. Louis as conquering heroes. People lined the rivers and roads as far as the eye could see to celebrate their homecoming.

President Jefferson called them to the capital to report the success of their mission. Captain Lewis submitted the official roll of the expedition with comments on each man's performance of duties and recommended the men be rewarded for their commitment and sacrifice. Congress and President Jefferson granted each double pay and 320 acres of land for their services. But York's name did not appear on the official roster. He received no pay, no land, and no recognition for his sacrifice.

In 1808 Clark moved to St. Louis to take up duties as chief Indian agent for the Territory of Upper Louisiana. As Clark's property, York was expected to go too. But York wanted to remain in Kentucky near his wife. He petitioned Clark for his freedom. Clark refused. It is unlikely that York ever saw his family again.

Ten years after the expedition returned, York was still enslaved by William Clark. Clark had ordered him beaten, jailed, and forced into hard labor in attempts to break York's continued desire to be free.

During an 1832 interview with famous writer Washington Irving, Clark said that he had eventually freed York. He claimed that he had set York up in a business hauling freight between Kentucky and Tennessee. Clark further claimed that York had failed miserably at the business and had died of cholera while trying to return to Clark. Official manumission papers, freeing York, have yet to be discovered.

That same year a group of trappers and fur traders reported that they had encountered a small party of Crow Indians. The group was led by a black man, their war chief, who told them that he had been to the ocean with Lewis and Clark.

Though we do not know for certain York's final fate, there are those among the Crow people who believe, without reservation, that York was one of them. If there is any justice in the world, I believe York found a home where he was looked at every day and called "Big Medicine."

Too few voices have been heard from the many people who helped build this great nation. Too many stories have been ignored. It is time to recognize this man, his voice, and his story, for the contribution and sacrifices he made.

His name was York.

HASAN DAVIS is an active speaker, trainer, and advocate for justice, education, and diversity initiatives at the local, state, and national levels. His active involvement in the Chautauqua—living history—education movement has garnered invitations to present his work at corporations, colleges, historical organizations, schools, prisons, and churches. Based in Kentucky, Hasan strives to build living and learning communities where all people have the opportunity to succeed. This is his first book for children.

ALLEANNA HARRIS earned a BFA in Animation from the University of the Arts in Philadelphia and graduated with honors. She is inspired by the beauty in everyday things and seeks to create images that are immersive, rich in color, and have a sense of warmth. When she's not illustrating, you can find Alleanna singing and dancing to her favorite music playlists, sharing her art on social media, researching history topics, and hanging with friends and family. She lives in New Jersey.

Thanks to our advisers for their expertise, research, and advice:

James J. Holmberg
Curator of Collections
The Filson Historical Society
Louisville, Kentucky

Katrina Phillips, Ph.D.
Assistant Professor, History Department
Macalester College
Saint Paul, Minnesota

The Journey of York is published by Capstone Editions
a Capstone imprint
1710 Roe Crest Drive
North Mankato, Minnesota 56003
www.capstonepub.com
Text copyright © 2019 Hasan Davis
Illustration copyright © 2019 by Capstone Editions, a Capstone imprint

Library of Congress Cataloging-in-Publication Data
Names: Davis, Hasan, author.
Title: The journey of York : the unsung hero of the Lewis and Clark
Expedition / by Hasan Davis.
Other titles: Unsung hero of the Lewis and Clark Expedition
Description: North Mankato, Minnesota : Capstone Editions, [2019] |
Series: Encounter: narrative nonfiction picture books. | Audience:
Ages 9-12.
Identifiers: LCCN 2017060429 (print) | LCCN 2018020305 (ebook) |
ISBN 9781543512908 (ebook PDF) | ISBN 9781543512823 (hardcover) |
ISBN 9781543512861 (paperback)
Subjects: LCSH: York, born approximately 1770- | Lewis and Clark
Expedition (1804-1806)—Juvenile literature. | African-American
explorers—Biography—Juvenile literature. | Explorers—Biography—
Juvenile literature. | African Americans—Relations with Indians—
Juvenile literature. | West (U.S.)—Discovery and exploration—Juvenile
literature.
Classification: LCC F592.7 (ebook) | LCC F592.7 .D37 2019 (print) |
DDC 910.92 [B] —dc23
LC record available at https://lccn.loc.gov/2017060429
Summary: Thomas Jefferson's Corps of Discovery included Captains
Lewis and Clark and a crew of 28 men to chart a route from St. Louis
to the Pacific Ocean. All the crew but one volunteered for the mission.
York, the enslaved man taken on the journey, did not choose to go.
York's contributions to the expedition, however, were invaluable.
The captains came to rely on York's judgement, determination, and
peacemaking role with the American Indian nations they encountered.
But as York's independence and status rose on the journey, the question
remained what status he would carry once the expedition was over.

Design Elements by Shutterstock: David M. Schrader (linen
texture), Taigi (old paper background)

Select Bibliography
Books:
Betts, Robert B. *In Search of York: The Slave Who Went to the
Pacific with Lewis and Clark, Revised Edition.* Boulder, CO:
University Press of Colorado, 2002.

Holmberg, James J., ed. *Dear Brother: Letters of William Clark to
Jonathan Clark.* New Haven, CT: Yale University Press, 2003.

Websites:
Jefferson, Thomas. "Jefferson's Instructions to Meriwether
Lewis." Washington, June 20, 1803. https://www.monticello.
org/site/jefferson/jeffersons-instructions-to-meriwether-lewis
Accessed on July 10, 2018.

"Journals of the Lewis and Clark Expedition." 1803–1806.
https://lewisandclarkjournals.unl.edu/journals/contents
Accessed July 10, 2018.

The Journey of York is based on the author's extensive research
of official documents, diaries, and correspondence from the era.
Every effort has been made to tell York's story with historical
accuracy, but the author has taken some creative license in
filling in the gaps, especially regarding the thoughts and
feelings of York, for which little to no historical
documentation exists.